LIVING WITH WOLVES!

True Stories of Adventures With Animals

Jim and Jamie Dutcher

NATIONAL GEOGRAPHIC

SCHOLASTIC INC.

ISBN 978-1-338-13256-4

12 11 10 9 8 7 6 5 4 3 2 1   17 18 19 20 21 22

Printed in the U.S.A.   40

First Scholastic printing, February 2017

Contributing writer: Moira Rose Donohue
Designer: Ruth Ann Thompson
Art director: Sanjida Rashid

Table of CONTENTS

KAMOTS: Howling With Wolves!   6

Chapter 1: Sign of the Wolf   8

Chapter 2: Leader of the Pack   18

Chapter 3: Cry Wolf   28

LAKOTA AND MATSI: My Bodyguard!   36

Chapter 1: Class Clown   38

Chapter 2: Once Bitten, Twice Shy   48

Chapter 3: You've Got a Friend   58

CHEMUKH: Cinderella Wolf!   68

Chapter 1: Look Into My Eyes   70

Chapter 2: Happy Birthday!   80

Chapter 3: New Pups on the Block   90

DON'T MISS!   99

Index and More Information   110

The Sawtooth Pack Family History

FIRST LITTER OF PUPS

KAMOTS – *"Freedom"*
(male)

LAKOTA – *"Friend"*
(male, brother to Kamots)

MOTAKI – *"Shadow"*
(female)

AIPUYI – *"One Who Speaks a Lot"*
(female)

SECOND LITTER OF PUPS

AMANI – *"Speaks the Truth"*
(male)

MOTOMO – *"He Who Goes First"*
(male)

MATSI – *"Sweet and Brave"*
(male)

THIRD LITTER OF PUPS

CHEMUKH – *"Black"*
(female)

WAHOTS – *"Likes to Howl"*
(male)

WYAKIN – *"Spirit Guide"*
(female, sister to Wahots)

FOURTH LITTER
THE SAWTOOTH PUPS
All Brothers and Sisters

PIYIP – *"Boy"*
(male)

AYET – *"Girl"*
(female)

MOTAKI – *"Shadow"*
(female)

KAMOTS: HOWLING WITH WOLVES!

These wolves join together for a group howl.

A wolf crouches low in a meadow to avoid being spotted.

SIGN of the WOLF

I was 16 years old when I first looked into the golden eyes of a gray wolf. I was working as a cowboy on a ranch in Wyoming. I was rounding up a herd of horses just as the sun was coming up. Suddenly, the horses became jittery. They pawed the ground. I felt a prickle on the back of my neck. And that's when I saw him. He was standing across the meadow, watching me.

I sat atop my horse, watching him. Slowly we circled each other. He seemed curious. I was curious, too. We stared at each other for minutes. Then the wolf turned and trotted off.

My name is Jim Dutcher. I've always been interested in how animals live. That's why I make films about wild animals. I've made movies about sea turtles, beavers, and cougars. After I finished the film about cougars, I needed a new idea. I decided to go back to that ranch in Wyoming.

I scrambled up a rocky mountain and looked around. Just like before, I felt like something, or someone, was watching me. I looked down to the rocky ledge (sounds like LEHJ) below me. Sure enough, a wolf was standing there. Like the wolf I had seen long ago, he stared at me. And I stared back. Then he disappeared.

This has to be a sign, I thought. *My next movie should be about wolves.*

Before I could start filming, I had to do my homework. I needed to learn about wolves. I read books and spoke to experts. I learned that the adult male gray wolf weighs between 70 and 130 pounds (32–59 kg). I was surprised to find out that wild wolves only live for about five years. But the most important thing I discovered is that wolves are social (sounds like SOH-shul) animals. They live in packs. Packs are a lot like human families. That gave me an idea. I would film the day-to-day life of a pack.

The Big Bad Wolf

Wolves in fairy tales are mean and scary. In "Little Red Riding Hood," the wolf eats Grandma. Then he tries to trick Little Red Riding Hood so he can eat her, too! Wolves are smart. But they rarely attack people. Bears and cougars are more dangerous to people, but even they rarely attack without cause. In the past 100 years, only two people were possibly killed by wolves in North America. And those stories about people turning into wolves? They're just made up. There are no such things as werewolves!

But wolves usually hide from people. They like their privacy. And they like to roam. Wolves walk at a rate of about 5 miles an hour (8 km/h). But when they are chasing prey, they can run 35 miles an hour (56 km/h) or faster. They can cover a lot of distance in a day—sometimes 50 miles (80 km)! To make a good film about these shy animals, I'd need a special plan.

Other people had studied wolves in small areas—less than 3 acres (1.2 ha). That was too small. It wouldn't give the wolves enough privacy and room to roam. I wanted the animals to be themselves so that I could see what their lives were really like. To do that, I figured I needed at least 25 acres (10.1 ha). That's about the size of 15 soccer fields! And I had to find just the right spot, too. It took me almost a year of searching to find it. One day, I stood in a meadow in Idaho. I looked around in all directions. I saw forests, a stream, and the snow-covered mountains of the Sawtooth Range.

"This is perfect," I whispered. The land was part of a national forest. The U.S. government said I could use it for my project. I gathered a three-person crew. We built a tall fence around the area. It took a lot of work to fence in such a big area.

Building a wolf territory was only part of my plan. To see how the wolves lived, I had to live with the wolves. My crew and I put up several tents, including a special tent called a yurt (sounds like YERT). A yurt is a round tent. It has a roof shaped like an upside-down ice-cream cone to help snow slide off. That would be handy in the winter.

Electricity would have been handy, too. But this was the wilderness. We would have to use candles and a wood stove. We had no running water. And we had no bathroom. We had to build an old-fashioned outhouse. Finally, with wolves living all around us, we'd need to fence in the tents so the wolves wouldn't steal our gear at night.

All that was missing now was the wolves. How would I find them? The last time wolves were seen in the Sawtooth mountains was 50 years ago.

"I'll have to start my own pack," I said to my crew. "Let's call it the Sawtooth Pack." I hoped that if I raised the wolves from pups, they would trust me. Then I would be able to photograph them up close. But I knew that if they trusted me, they would never be able to live in the wild. People hunt wolves. And ranchers sometimes kill wolves to protect their livestock. That's why wolves hide. I would have to plan for that later.

Finding wolf pups isn't easy. I scoured wolf research centers and eventually found four pups. They were all newborns. Two were brothers, and they looked alike. I named them Kamots (sounds like ka-MAHTS) and Lakota (sounds like la-KOH-tah). Kamots means "freedom" in the Blackfoot Indian language. Lakota means "friend" in Lakota-Sioux.

The other two were females. One was very dark. I named her Motaki (sounds like moh-TAH-key). That means "shadow" in Blackfoot. The other one made a lot of noise. I called her Aipuyi (sounds like eye-POO-ee), which means "one who speaks a lot."

I knew that they were too young to live alone in the camp. I made them a small pen in the yurt. I thought I could live my normal life while I was taking care of them. Boy, was I wrong! They had to be fed every four to six hours. They guzzled formula from bottles. I called in my family and crew. Together, we fed the wiggly pups. With all that eating, the pups grew quickly. Within a month or two, they weighed 20 pounds (9 kg)! They were curious about everything. But *one* pup was more curious than the others.

As a puppy, Kamots was very curious. Here he nibbles on a log to see what it tastes like.

LEADER of the PACK

Kamots wanted to explore everything. He and the other pups blew through the tent like little hurricanes. They snatched clothes, straps, tools, shoes—anything that wasn't nailed down. In minutes, they had chewed them to bits!

It was time for them to move out of the tent. But they were still too small for the big territory.

"What should we do with them?"
I asked my crew. "They need a safe place."
Then I figured it out. We fenced in an area
just outside the yurt. That way we could
keep an eye on them. And there would be
fewer things for them to chew on. Of
course, there was always the bottom of my

shirt to nibble. And
sometimes … *Ouch!*
That was my finger!

Within a few
months, I knew they
were ready for the big
enclosure. I felt like
I was sending my kids
off to school for the first time. I fumbled
with the latch while the pups jumped up
and whined with excitement. I opened the

Did You Know?

A wolf has 42 very sharp, curved teeth. These help the wolf hold on to its prey. The wolf's canine teeth can be an inch (2.5 cm) long.

gate, and they charged out. Guess who was right out in front? Kamots.

Kamots was fearless. He hopped onto a log and walked along it, like a tight-rope walker. When he was tired of that game, he wanted down. Jumping off was scarier than hopping on. But he only hesitated for a second. I could see that he had the gift of confidence.

The other pups followed Kamots around like he was in charge. I wasn't really surprised. I had noticed that Kamots was braver and more curious right from the start—a natural leader.

Every wolf pack needs a leader. The lead wolf is called the alpha (sounds like AL-fuh). He's like the captain of a ship. He goes first when they explore. If he senses danger, he makes sure the other wolves are safe before taking care of himself.

Before long, I saw other signs that Kamots was the alpha wolf. He howled first, keeping his head higher than the others when he did. *Arroooo!* And he was the first to greet human visitors. But the most astonishing sign came as soon as I began feeding the wolves like they were in the wild.

I fed them raw meat every three to five days. I talked to local officials. They allowed me to find dead animals that had been hit by cars. That way they wouldn't go to waste, and the wolves would have food to eat. Kamots ran to the food first.

But when the other wolves tried to join him, he glared at them and bared his teeth.

He snarled and flattened his ears. Even his brother, Lakota, had to wait his turn. I was shocked to see Kamots act like this. But then I understood. The alpha says who eats when. By telling the other wolves to wait, Kamots was telling them that he was in charge.

When Kamots growled at the others, he was acting like a parent scolding a child. There are a lot of ways a wolf pack is like a family. I once heard about a wolf that was kicked in the jaw by a moose. His jaw was broken, and he couldn't chew meat. His pack chewed up food and fed it to him. Like a human family, they took care of a hurt member.

Arroooo!

Wolves howl for a lot of reasons. It doesn't seem to matter if the moon is out or not. Why do they howl? Sometimes it's to call to each other. Sometimes it's because they have a full belly. Often they howl because they enjoy it—it's like singing for them. Each wolf has a unique sound. We learned to identify which wolf was howling. We thought that Lakota had the prettiest howl. Wolves start howling when they are pups. But it sounds more like yodeling!

Only once did I ever see Kamots outsmarted. It was at dinnertime. And it took two wolves to do it. One wolf crept up, snatched a very small piece of meat and scampered off. His partner in crime waited his turn. As soon as Kamots ran after the first wolf with the meat, the second wolf lunged and grabbed a bigger chunk of meat. The second wolf raced off in the opposite direction. Kamots saw him out of the corner of his eye and chased him. Meanwhile, the first wolf ran back to dinner and grabbed an even larger hunk. Kamots never fell for this trick again!

Every morning, the wolves greeted each other. First, they licked Kamots on the face. Then they licked each other. They greeted me the same way. Once a wolf got his tooth stuck up my nose somehow. *Ugh—that was weird!* After the morning greeting, the wolves would wander off.

In the evenings, the wolves often threw their heads back and howled. It was their version of singing songs around a campfire. The sound was ghostly and beautiful. Usually Kamots would start it. Then the others joined. Sometimes I did, too.

Pretty soon, Kamots was a full-grown alpha wolf. But I wasn't afraid of him.

We trusted each other. Maybe he understood that I was the leader—the alpha—of my human film crew. I never approached the wolves first. I always waited for Kamots and the others to approach me. And I made sure my crew didn't treat them like pet dogs. I needed to see the wolves acting like wolves.

I filmed them often. I took pictures of wolves playing in the meadow. I filmed them pawing at bubbles under the ice in a frozen stream. I wanted to film them at night. It was exciting to watch them eating in the dark, eyes glowing. But I needed light to do that. And we had no electricity.

Our lights from inside make the yurt seem to glow.

To get the electricity we needed, I got a small generator (sounds like JEN-uh-ray-tore). It would make enough power to light a lamp. I put the lamp 20 feet (6 m) up in a tree.

"Help me run this power cord up the tree." I asked my daughter, Christina, to help.

That night, I filmed the wolves and then took the light down. But I

left the cord wrapped high in the tree.
The next morning, we noticed bits of
something orange in the snow. "What
happened here?" Christina asked. Wolves
happened. Overnight, they had torn up the
power cord! We never knew how they
could reach the cord so high in the tree.
They were very clever!

Soon, the wolves were adults. I thought
it was time to add to the pack. It was
springtime, and before long I found three
more pups. I named them Amani (sounds
like uh-MAH-nee), Motomo (sounds like
moh-TOE-moh), and Matsi (sounds like
MAHT-zee). Matsi means "sweet and
brave," and he lived up to his name.

When the time came to introduce the
pups to the pack, all the adult wolves

danced at the
fence. Wolves love
puppies. The wolves
welcomed the pups
with licks and whines.

Then Kamots showed me
how an alpha acts with pups. He took
charge. He held his tail high to signal to
the pups that he was the leader. The other
wolves stood aside. Kamots led the young
wolves on a tour of the territory.

Then it was dinnertime. Kamots ran
up to the food first, as usual. The puppies
smelled the food and bounded up. *Uh-oh!*
I held my breath. These pups were about
to learn an important lesson. But I was
wrong. Kamots allowed them to feast with
him. He seemed to know that they needed

to eat so they would grow and become strong for winter.

Kamots was always interested in what I was doing. I was filming in the snow one day. I pulled my raincoat over my camera to protect it. Kamots found my raincoat irresistible (sounds like ih-ree-ZIS-tah-bul). He sneaked up next to me. I didn't notice him until he snatched my raincoat and ran off, shredding it as he went!

He was nosy about other people, too. One time, a visitor came into wolf camp. He was excited to see wolves up close.

He brought a camera and a video recorder with him. When the wolves came up to him, he put down his camera so he could film them. Within moments, Kamots and Matsi had grabbed the camera. *Chomp!*

A few weeks later, I found a chunk of plastic with some wires attached. I mailed it back to our guest with a note: "Kamots enjoyed your camera; he's finished with it now."

That's not all Kamots was curious about. He was fascinated (sounds like FAS-uh-nay-ted) by the hat I always wore. Kamots kept trying to slip it off my head. But I always managed to grab it just in time. One day, I pretended to be very busy with my camera. I felt Kamots get close. But I didn't reach for my hat. I let him rip it off my head.

Kamots acted like he had won the million-dollar prize. He pranced around, shaking and flipping it. And of course, I never saw it again!

Occasionally, Kamots would sit with me. One day, I was worried about the project. Things kept going wrong. And the wolves were hard to film. They would stick their snouts into the camera as soon as I lined up a good photo. Kamots joined me and sat close. He seemed to know I was sad. He rolled onto his side and slowly raised his paw. He held it out it out to me, paw pads forward. I sensed it was a gesture of comfort. I answered with my hand.

Soon after, I got some new ideas. One idea was to use a different camera lens so I could photograph the wolves from a distance. Another idea was to get the help of a friend. I had met Jamie years before. She liked animals as much as I did. She took care of sick and injured animals at the National Zoo in Washington, D.C. I invited her to join me at the camp.

Jamie arrived in the middle of winter. The snow was too deep to drive all the way. So we hiked the last mile into their territory. I took her to meet the wolves. I cupped my hands around my mouth. *Arroooo!* I howled to let the wolves know I had returned. One by one, they howled back. *Arroooo!*

Matsi and Lakota were friends.

LAKOTA AND MATSI: MY BODYGUARD!

Lakota (left) and Matsi (right) often played with each other.

Chapter 1

One day, I saw Motaki crouch down. She lowered her chest and stuck her rump in the air. Her body language said, "Playtime!" But the other wolves didn't want to play. So Motaki darted at them. She nipped gently. *Tag—you're it!* One by one, the other wolves joined the game. They chased after her. She jumped and ran, wagging her tail. She was happy.

Motaki was a beautiful wolf with dark fur. Despite their name, gray wolves come in different colors. Some are gray, but they can also be brown, beige (sounds like BAYJ), white, and even black. Most are not one solid color.

Motaki had joined the pack with Kamots and the first litter of pups. Kamots had been brave, right from the start. But Motaki was the opposite. She was always a timid pup. She never forged ahead into new places. And she always crouched the lowest to show her respect.

Once in a while, the other wolves would take out their frustrations (sounds like fruss-STRAY-shuns) on Motaki. They would snap and growl at her. But even so, the other wolves never seriously hurt

Motaki. From the time she was little, Motaki loved to play. She was always the one who started the games. Motaki was the omega (sounds like oh-MAY-gah) wolf of the Sawtooth Pack. The omega is the lowest-ranked wolf.

I had already seen that wolves ate by rank. That meant the alpha ate first. And the omega wolf ate last. Motaki always stood away from the food and watched the others eat. She licked her lips. I could tell she was hungry. Wolves don't eat every day. So every meal is important. But Motaki waited her turn. She knew her place.

The Better to Eat You With

What do wolves "wolf down" when they're hungry? Well, they don't eat nuts and berries. And they don't eat Grandma! They eat other wild animals. Wolves like to eat elk and deer and other large mammals. They also eat smaller prey, such as rabbits and mice. To kill large animals, they work as a team. They watch for weaker animals. They look for older animals, the sick or injured, or the very young. The faster wolves chase the animal. Then the strongest ones attack. Once the prey is caught, the wolves eat almost the whole thing.

Every now and then, Motaki got upset about always being last. Then she would wander off by herself. That's a dangerous thing to do. The pack protects its members. Alone, a wolf can be attacked by other predators (sounds like PRED-uh-ters).

One spring day, Motaki didn't show up for dinner. I waited and waited, but I knew something must be wrong. So I went to look for her. I was afraid there might be an opening in the fence. Sneaking off by myself, I walked along the entire fence. But there were no openings. I searched the enclosure. Behind some tall trees, I found her body. I felt so sad. Some animal had attacked her. I really wanted to know what animal had killed Motaki. I needed to make sure that the other wolves were safe.

But I had to be careful. The animal might still be nearby, and it might attack me! Slowly, I examined the area. And then I spied a clue—wolf claw marks around a tree trunk.

The wolves must have found Motaki before I did and smelled something in the tree. Wolves have a very strong sense of smell. They can sometimes sniff things 1.8 miles (2.8 km) away. Their sense of smell helps them hunt. The wolves must have clawed the tree trunk trying to reach the animal that attacked Motaki.

Now I had a pretty good guess what animal it was. I thought it must have been a cougar, also known as a mountain lion. I knew about cougars from the film I had made. They can climb trees.

Wolves sometimes kill cougars. But cougars are one of the few animals that can kill a wolf. Not only that, they lived in this part of the country. I thought I had kept the wolves safe with the fence. But a cougar must have climbed a nearby tree, then leaped over the electric wire and jumped in.

Did You Know?

Elk and moose are members of the deer family. But they're not the same animal. Elk are brown and have thin, pointed antlers. Moose are larger and have wide shovel-like antlers. Moose are blackish brown.

Sometime later in the spring, I was exploring outside the enclosure. Elk were ambling around. I also came upon tracks that were made by a cougar. Cougars eat elk, just like wolves do. They lurk in areas where elk are common. Had the cougar that attacked Motaki returned? Then I spied cougar prints near a tent that was outside the enclosure. Now I was worried about my crew, too. I kept following the tracks. I was scared. If the cougar was nearby, it could have been waiting to pounce on me! Luckily, I never saw it, and it never came back.

The pack acted differently after Motaki had been attacked. I could tell they missed her. And they missed having an omega.

They didn't have anyone to start their games. They seemed to have lost their spirit. All summer long, they just hung around. Sometimes, they seemed to be searching or waiting for her. I had heard once about a pack that walked in figure-eight patterns, searching for a member that had disappeared.

For at least six weeks, their howls sounded different, too. I thought they might be calling Motaki back. Often I heard only one wolf at a time. It always sounded sad.

I understood even more how much the pack needed an omega. *What could I do to cheer them up?* I wondered. That's when I got the idea to add more pups! I knew that wolves love puppies. It was time to grow the pack. So that's how the second litter— Amani, Matsi, and Motomo—came to join the pack.

Kamots disciplines his brother Lakota.

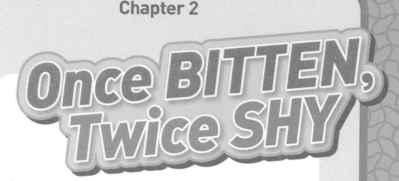

Once BITTEN, Twice SHY

Having three new pups join the pack certainly helped cheer up the adult wolves. But it wasn't enough. The wolves still needed an omega. Age doesn't determine a wolf's rank in the pack. So the fact that the pups weren't full grown didn't impact their ability to be an omega. Size doesn't matter, either. Rank in a wolf pack is set by the wolves' personalities.

The first letter of the Greek alphabet is alpha. Beta is the second letter, and the last letter is omega. People often use the Greek letters to describe animals' roles in their families.

Lakota looked a lot like his alpha brother, Kamots, only a little bigger. But like many human brothers, they had different personalities. Kamots was a leader from the start. But Lakota had always been shy. He was timid and fearful. He was afraid of new things and loud noises. As a pup, Kamots explored and charged ahead into new places. Lakota often stayed behind.

Sometime after the pups arrived, I noticed that the adult wolves began to argue among themselves. They snarled and bared their teeth. They jumped on one another. They weren't fighting. They were using wolf body language. Wolves show their feelings with physical signs. A direct stare says, "I'm in charge." A wagging tail means the wolf is excited. Lips curled back is a warning.

Wolves also communicate by how they stand. I could tell that each one of the wolves was trying to show that he was stronger and more dominant (sounds like DAH-mi-nent) than the others. Although the omega is an important job, none of the wolves wanted to be on the bottom.

One day, the wolves began an argument over food. Wolves can gobble up a lot when they find food. Sometimes they can eat 22 pounds (10 kg) at a time. That's about one-fifth of their total body weight!

Suddenly, one wolf lunged at Lakota and pushed him away from the meat. Poor

Lakota crouched down. He was hungry. And he knew that if he got cut off from the food, his rank as bottom wolf could be set. He sneaked back in, crawling on his belly. This time, a different wolf snapped at him. But Lakota didn't try to fight back—he was too gentle. Instead, he turned his eyes to his brother. Without his brother's help, Lakota didn't stand a chance. He whined. *Protect me!* he seemed to be saying.

But Kamots didn't protect Lakota. Kamots was the leader. He knew that the pack needed a new omega. And just like that, over dinner, Lakota was forced into his new role.

Not long after, a wolf jumped on top of Lakota. Lakota dropped to the ground and rolled on his side. He tucked his tail and licked the other wolf's muzzle. That's how he showed his respect. The other wolf left him alone.

A few days later, it happened again. This time several wolves piled on top of Lakota. No matter how low he crouched, they growled and nipped at him. There was no doubt about it—he was the new omega.

I hated to see him bullied. But like Kamots had done, I had to stand aside and let it happen.

Lakota accepted his role for the good of the family. He seemed to know it was important to have a healthy pack. Like Motaki before him, Lakota did his best to start games with the wolves. He would run off and try to get someone to follow. I even saw him get his brother to roughhouse (sounds like RUFF-hous) with him! Lakota darted at Kamots. Kamots turned and followed. They raced through the meadow, chasing each other. Then they jumped up on their hind legs and wrestled. Finally, Lakota let himself be caught. Kamots stood over him. The game was over.

Even though they played together, Kamots kept Lakota in his place. One day, Lakota tried to eat before his turn. He crouched down, trying to get as low as he could. Then he tiptoed closer, hoping the other wolves were too busy eating to notice.

But Kamots noticed. He lifted up his head, curled back his lips, and showed his teeth. *Grrrr!* A growl rumbled in the back of his throat. Then he lunged at Lakota and chased him away.

High Four

A wolf's front paws are larger than its back paws. The average front paw is about four inches (10 cm) long and five inches (12.7 cm) wide. That's almost as big as an adult's hand! Each paw has four toes that touch the ground. Their toes are slightly webbed, like a duck's foot. Coarse hair grows in between the toes. These features act like built-in snowshoes so wolves can walk on top of snow. Wolves walk and run on their toes, which makes them fast.

When Lakota came back, he flipped onto his back. Kamots stood over him, his paws on both sides of Lakota, keeping him in place. Lakota had to wait.

Lakota had adjusted to his role in the pack by the time Jamie arrived at wolf camp. When I introduced Jamie to the wolves, Kamots approached her first. The other wolves waited. He sniffed her and then licked her. Then the other wolves crowded around her. They licked every part of Jamie's face. She was thrilled. Of course, she had to keep her mouth shut, or they would lick inside, too!

But one wolf stayed back. "Why doesn't that wolf come to me?" she asked, pointing to Lakota. She knew that wolves are naturally afraid of people. But these wolves were used to living with humans.

"He's the omega," I said. "If the others see him getting attention, they will attack him." Like me, Jamie felt bad for Lakota.

The next day, we went for a walk around wolf camp. We plodded through the heavy snow in our snowshoes. At one point, we turned around. Several wolves were following us. I knew they were trying to figure out who this new person was.

I hoped we might come across Lakota, but he was hiding. Jamie and I went back toward the yurt. We plopped down in the snow. I was starting to worry about Lakota. Then we heard something in the bushes nearby. *Swish!* I held my breath. *Oh, no! Was the cougar back?*

Jamie and Lakota formed a special bond.

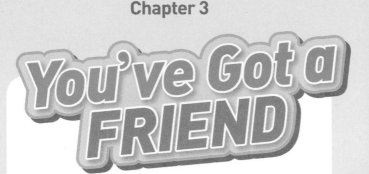

Chapter 3

You've Got a FRIEND

Swish! We heard the sound again. The bush shook, and an animal poked its nose out. It was Lakota! He'd been waiting for us. With his tail tucked and his head down, he inched toward Jamie. He licked her face.

"Hello, Lakota," she said. She ruffled his fur. "Nice to finally meet you." Lakota sat down next to her and placed his paw on her shoulder.

He stayed that way for a while. Jamie fell in love.

Jamie had joined me and the wolves in the middle of the winter. Winters in the Sawtooth mountains are freezing! The area can get six feet (1.8 m) or more of snow each year. This year was colder than usual. Jamie and I spent a lot of time shoveling snow off the roof of the tents.

But snow doesn't bother wolves. They dive into it. They play in it. They're rarely cold. That's because wolves have a double layer of fur. Their outer fur is longer and blocks the wind. It can be more than one color. And they often have dark markings on their body and faces. Underneath, they have a thick, woolly coat that keeps them warm. No matter what color the outer coat is, a gray wolf's undercoat is always a dull gray. Without a furry undercoat, all Jamie and I could do was bundle up in layers. Sometimes we wore two pairs of gloves!

Jamie got to know the wolves quickly. Matsi, Motomo, and Amani were from the same litter. But they each looked different. Matsi was a beige wolf. His face didn't have the dark markings of most wolves. He stood out for other reasons, too. The wolves from this newest litter weren't fully grown yet, but they were showing their own special personalities. Matsi wasn't timid, like Lakota. He wasn't a leader, like Kamots. But he was bold and lively. And he was gentle and sweet.

"I've been watching Matsi's behavior," I told Jamie. "I think he's showing signs of becoming the beta (sounds like BAY-tuh) wolf." The beta wolf is the second-in-command. He's like the captain's first mate. In our pack, the beta helped keep order in the pack. He was the peacekeeper. When new pups joined the pack, the beta was also the puppy-sitter. He taught the pups the rules of wolf behavior (sounds like bee-HAYV-yur).

At last, it was spring. Flowers bloomed in the meadow. Now it was easier to walk around the camp and check on the wolves. We could even watch the wolves from the raised deck of the yurt. That's when we began to notice Amani's behavior.

Amani seemed to pick on Lakota more than the others. The young wolf would grab Lakota's fur in his jaw and tug extra hard! Then he would jump on Lakota. Over the next few months, his play got even rougher.

Matsi was always right in the middle of the action. Like the others, he would chase Lakota away from the food if Lakota tried to sneak a taste early. But Matsi didn't join Amani and the other wolves in picking on Lakota. In fact, Matsi just watched. We were puzzled.

Then something surprising happened. I was filming the wolves. They had come together to howl. One of the wolves got annoyed with Lakota. That was enough to get Amani started. He nipped Lakota. Then he and the others ganged up on Lakota.

Side by Side

Today, dogs are "man's best friends." The friendship started thousands of years ago. Some people think wolves followed hunters and snacked on their leftovers. But it may have been the other way around. Today, some Ethiopian wolves have been hanging out with a troop of large ground-dwelling monkeys in Africa. These monkeys are called geladas (sounds like juh-LAH-duhs). Normally wolves would eat baby monkeys. But these wolves are eating rodents instead. Are the wolves hiding among the monkeys to hunt for other prey? Or are they becoming friends with the monkeys?

Snarling, they surrounded him. Lakota must have been scared. He dropped down to make himself smaller. He tried to slink away. Amani wouldn't let him.

Suddenly, Matsi charged in. His teeth were bared. Fur flew. Amani stopped short. He backed off. A moment later, the group broke up. Lakota crawled away. I had caught it all on film. I wanted Jamie to look at what had happened.

"I was really surprised to see Matsi attack Lakota," I said. "Maybe he was just keeping the peace," Jamie suggested. "Can you rewind the film and play it again?"

We watched the film again in slow motion. That's when Jamie spotted something. Matsi had rushed in, snapping. But he wasn't biting at Lakota.

"Look!" Jamie cried. "Matsi's biting Amani, not Lakota! He knocked Amani away from Lakota. That's why the fight stopped so quickly." Jamie was right. Matsi had put himself between Amani and Lakota. That was dangerous. Matsi was brave. He was protecting Lakota!

Matsi had become Lakota's bodyguard. He had set limits for the wolves. They were not to play too rough with Lakota. If they did, they would have to answer to him, the beta wolf. It worked. Amani didn't bully Lakota too much if Matsi was there. We saw something else, too. Matsi and Lakota liked to go off by themselves together.

In the summer, they rolled in the grass with each other and went exploring. They would brush shoulders as they walked. It was a way of saying to each other, *I'm still here.*

Lakota relaxed when Matsi was there. He jumped up and put his paws on Matsi's shoulders. They wrestled, but no one got hurt. Lakota wagged his tail when they played. And at night, Matsi and Lakota often curled up together.

Years later, a new wolf in the pack would become the omega. Sometimes packs will let an omega retire if another one comes along. Lakota would become a mid-ranking wolf again. But Matsi and Lakota stayed best friends. No one knows why certain people become friends. It's the same with wolves.

Chemukh, with black fur, stands out in the middle of the pack.

CHEMUKH: CINDERELLA WOLF!

Wahots greets Jamie the wolf way. Jamie had to get used to being licked on the face!

Chapter 1

LOOK Into My EYES

My name is Jamie. I'm Jim Dutcher's wife. I helped photograph the wolves. And I recorded sounds for the films. Now Jim and I work together to teach people about wolves.

I've always loved animals. When I was little, I dreamed of living in the woods behind my house. I imagined making friends with the bears. I didn't, of course. But when

I grew up, I got a job at the hospital at the National Zoo in Washington, D.C. I took care of sick and hurt animals. I enjoyed my work. But I was very happy when Jim invited me to join him at wolf camp. It was my chance to live with animals. My dream was coming true.

I was excited when Jim said it was time to add more pups. Silly me—I didn't know what I was getting into! I had seen how intelligent wolves were. And I knew they were curious. But I hadn't imagined the mischief those little pups could cause. Everything was a toy to them—gloves, a box of cookies, even trash.

We named the new pups Wahots (sounds like wuh-HOTZ), Wyakin (sounds like why-AH-kin), and Chemukh (sounds like sha-MOOK). Wahots, whose name means "likes to howl" and Wyakin ("spirit guide") were brother and sister. Chemukh was a female but not from the same litter. Her fur was black.

Wyakin and Wahots had a special bond from the start. Chemukh was more timid and kept to herself. Sometimes Wyakin and Wahots plotted together and ganged up on Chemukh. Chemukh was the odd one out. Maybe that's why she often came to me.

The pups were rascals. One day Wyakin grabbed a rag I was using to clean her with. She snarled viciously when

Did You Know?

A wolf can bite with the force of 1,500 pounds per square inch (150 kg/sq cm). A wolf's bite can crush the thighbone of a moose.

I tried to take it back. So I scolded her like her mother wolf would. I flipped her onto her back. *Grrrr!* I growled. She let go right away.

Before long, the third litter was old enough to join the adult wolves. We opened the gate, and Wyakin and Wahots walked out.

They were a little shy. Then Kamots marched up to them and licked them. They relaxed and the other wolves rushed in to greet them. Wahots and Wyakin started a game of tug-of-war. Matsi, the beta wolf, joined them. He let them nibble his ear.

But little Chemukh stayed behind. She

watched from the puppy pen. Finally, she entered her new home but ran off to hide. After about an hour, she tiptoed out. She approached the other pups and started to play with them. Jim and I were relieved.

"I think that's enough for today," Jim said. We were tired from the excitement of introducing the pups to the pack. I put my sound recording equipment away. Suddenly, I heard whining behind me. *Had timid Chemukh followed me back into the puppy area?* I turned around. I was surprised to see that somehow little Wahots was shut in with me!

I went to open the gate for Wahots. Gentle Matsi was waiting on the other side to take Wahots back to the pack. As the beta wolf, Matsi often looked after the pups. He taught them to show respect to the adults by rolling onto their backs. Later, he would teach them to wait to eat. For now, he made sure no one pushed them away from the food.

When Wyakin was still in the puppy camp, she had a funny habit. She would take a chunk of meat and sneak off to her puppy bed. She would hide it there and come back to eat with the other pups. Then later, she would look for the hidden snack. But it was never there. Her brother had figured out her trick. He ate it when she wasn't looking. When they joined the pack, Wyakin continued her food-hiding tricks. But when she searched for it, the food was always gone. Wyakin never figured out who was taking her food!

Wolves and the Ecosystem

Every animal plays a part in the balance of nature. People killed almost all the wolves in the western United States nearly 100 years ago. This changed the balance of wildlife in areas where wolves had lived. For example, without wolves, the elk population grew. Elk spread out along the rivers and streams. They munched on young trees and willows there. Without the shade from the trees, the water grew warmer. That was not a healthy place for fish to live. When the wolves were returned, the elk needed to look for a safe place to live. They moved away from the rivers. In many places, trees grew back, water became cooler, and balance was restored.

One day, something changed at mealtime. Kamots chased Chemukh away from the food. He made her wait to eat. Matsi couldn't step in to help her. We never knew why Kamots acted like this. But we think it was because of Chemukh's lack of confidence. As he expected, she didn't challenge him. In larger packs, sometimes there are two omegas—one male and one female. We thought that Chemukh was on the road to becoming the female omega.

Then things changed again. Chemukh and Wyakin became mature female wolves. Usually in a pack only the alpha male and alpha female mate. And they mate for life. So only Kamots and one of the females would have pups. Chemukh and Wyakin would have to compete to be the alpha female.

Suddenly, shy little Chemukh started pushing Wyakin around. She nipped at Wyakin and knocked her down. She bit Wyakin's leg.

If she were a person, you would probably call her a "mean girl." She didn't mind that it made her unpopular with the other wolves. She just wanted to make sure Kamots saw her. Kamots watched. At first, he didn't get involved. But one day, he looked only at Chemukh.

Kamots chose Chemukh to be the alpha female.

Chapter 2

HAPPY BIRTHDAY!

Chemukh held Kamots's stare. They stood looking into each other's eyes for a long time. Then Kamots turned, and Chemukh followed. He had picked her to be his mate.

Cinderella had won the heart of the prince. And just like that, Chemukh went from nearly being the omega female to being crowned the alpha female.

The alpha male and the alpha female are like the parents of a family. Kamots let the other wolves know that she would eat with him. He protected her from the other wolves. He was sweet and gentle with her.

"I thought that Kamots would pick Wyakin," said Jim. "Me too," I said. "Why do you think he chose Chemukh?"

We talked about it. We remembered that Kamots had been the first one to push Chemukh away from the food. Had he changed his mind and decided he liked her? "Maybe he saw her competitive spirit," Jim suggested. By challenging Wyakin, Chemukh showed Kamots that she could be strong.

Before long, Chemukh needed to find a den before her pups were born. A wolf's den is like a small cave. Usually it's in a deep hole. Wolves often look for a fallen log. Then they dig under the log to make a cozy den. Chemukh spent weeks looking for just the right place. It had to shelter the newborns from the weather and from other animals.

Chemukh was very picky. She would find a spot and dig a bit. Then she would stop. Too rocky. She would find another place and dig. Too wet.

Finally, she found a place that was just right. It was near a cluster of tall spruce trees. One tree had fallen, so there was a cave-like area under it. Chemukh disappeared into it. Soon dirt was flying everywhere. She dug on and off for several days. The other wolves got so excited when they saw her digging, they started to dig holes of their own, too. Jim and I were also excited, but we didn't dig any holes!

What we were most excited about was that, unlike the wolves we had raised, these would be the first pups born to the Sawtooth Pack. And they would be the first wolves to be born in the Sawtooth mountains in at least 50 years. Hunters had been killing off wolves for many years. In the mid-1800s, there had been hundreds of thousands of wolves in the United States. But over time, their numbers dropped. Some ranchers killed them, too, thinking they were protecting their livestock. Some people hunted wolves for sport or because they were afraid. Many more did it because the government wanted to get rid of wolves.

What You Can Do to Help

In the 1990s, the U.S. government started bringing wolves back. Soon, there were a few thousand. Sadly, some states have allowed people to hunt wolves in large numbers again. You can help protect them. First, learn as much as you can about wolves. Then share what you know. Give a presentation to your class or to a group of friends and family. The more people know, the more they'll love wolves, too. Finally, you can help raise money. Giving the money to groups that are working to save wolves, such as Living With Wolves, can help.

There was a lot about wolves people didn't understand. That led to problems. And by the 1960s, there were only around 370 wolves left in the United States outside of Alaska. We hoped our pack would help people learn and care about wolves. We were learning so much from watching our wolves, and we couldn't wait to share what we'd seen. We were especially excited to learn more about what happens when pups are born.

It was a frosty cold April day. Snow coated the meadow. Chemukh slipped quietly away from the pack. At first, we didn't even notice. Neither did the wolves.

When we got up the next morning, it was very quiet. "Where are the wolves?" I asked. "Do you think—?" asked Jim.

We threw on our clothes and walked quietly to the den. Sure enough, the wolves were all there. They were racing and pacing and prancing. They whined outside the den. They sniffed the air for the smell of pups.

We felt their excitement, but we didn't want to get too close. Then we heard a wonderful sound. *We-oooo, we-oooo, we-oooo!* Tiny whines floated out from the den. The pups had arrived!

Wolves usually have between four and six pups in a litter. Wolf pups are born deaf and blind. They weigh about one pound (0.5 kg). That's about the same as a loaf of bread. At two weeks, they open their eyes. Their eyes are blue. They change to yellow later. At about three weeks, their ears start to stand up. And they can start to hear.

At first, wolf pups drink only their mother's milk. Then in about three weeks, they start to get their teeth. That's when they start wanting real food! But they're not old enough to eat meat the way the adults do. So their mother will regurgitate (sounds like ree-GUR-jih-tate), or throw up, already eaten food for the pups to snack on. Food that is already chewed is easier for the pups to swallow. It sounds disgusting, but the pups gobble it up!

No one was allowed in the den—not even the new dad, Kamots. Over the next few days, however, the wolves were allowed to peek in from the doorway. Wyakin stayed

Did You Know?

When wolf pups are ready to eat regurgitated food, they will lick their mother's muzzle.

by the opening. She was like an aunt. She was there to help Chemukh.

I was desperate to see the pups, just like the wolves. Chemukh and I had a special relationship that started when she was little. Even after she joined the other wolves, she still spent a lot of time with me. Unlike Lakota, she never worried that the other wolves would pick on her for getting my attention. Maybe she just felt closer to me because I am female, too. We trusted each other. *But would that get me a backstage pass now?* I wondered.

A few days after the pups were born, I decided to put our trust to the test. Maybe I was reckless, or maybe I was brave. I suspect I was a little of both. I really wanted to see the pups.

Two of Chemukh and Kamots's pups cautiously peek out of the den.

Chapter 3

NEW PUPS on the BLOCK

As I approached the den, Jim stayed close by to make sure I was okay. After all, I was about to enter a wolf den! I sat down at the opening and waited. Chemukh popped her head out and stared at me. Then she crawled out, whined and licked me on the nose.

"Congratulations on your new pups," I whispered. "Would you let me look at them?" I kept my voice soft and gentle. I pulled a small flashlight out of my pocket and held it out to her so she could sniff it.

Chemukh cocked her head. Then she moved away from the opening. I decided that was an invitation. I rolled onto my hands and knees and crept to the entrance. It wasn't very wide. As I squeezed under the log, I wondered if I might get stuck. That would be embarrassing. Then I realized that I might get bitten on my behind by Chemukh. That would be a lot worse!

I slowly shimmied into the narrow tunnel. I didn't want to scare Chemukh. I slithered through the five-foot (1.5-m)-long dirt tunnel on my belly like a giant snake. It was dark and damp. Small roots hung down from the ceiling.

Mother wolves are very protective of their babies. A wolf in Yellowstone National Park once held off giant grizzly bears to keep them from snatching her pups!

I thought it would be smelly, but it wasn't. Chemukh kept it clean. She knew that if it had any odor, it would attract predators.

I was getting closer. I could hear the pups chirping. I turned on my flashlight. The tunnel turned left, and the floor sloped upward. I had read that wolves make the end of the tunnel higher. That way, they can make sure the pups stay above any water that might trickle in.

There they were. I could see three little heads. They looked like tiny bear cubs. They stuck their noses in the air to sniff me. Or maybe they thought I was going to feed them!

"Oh, you're so cute," I told them. "And don't worry, your mom is just outside." They whined back at me. I knew better than to touch them. So I just looked for a minute and then started to back out slowly.

I moved carefully. I didn't want to do anything that would upset Chemukh. I wriggled out of the tunnel. Chemukh was waiting. She looked calm, and I relaxed. I praised her pups and smiled. Chemukh licked my dirty face. Then she disappeared back into the den to check on the pups. It was a moment I will never forget.

We brought food in for the pack, as usual. Chemukh didn't join the other wolves to eat. She stayed in the den and waited, acting like a queen. Kamots dragged an entire deer leg to the den entrance for her.

Wyakin brought food to her as well. Maybe it was the food she usually hid!

A few weeks passed. The pups could see and walk now, and Chemukh was ready to show them to the pack. One by one she brought three healthy pups out of the den. She carried them gently in her mouth by the backs of their necks and placed them in a dry, sunny patch.

They tottered on wobbly legs. The pups were all black, like their mother. The adult wolves greeted the pups with licks and sniffs and gentle nudges. They were excited but made sure they didn't hurt the little ones.

Over the next few weeks, the wolves were anxious (sounds like ANGK-shuhs) to pitch in to help with the pups. Wyakin helped groom them when Chemukh went off to eat. And of course, Matsi spent time with them. He took his role as babysitter and teacher very seriously, as he had with the other pups. After all, these little pups had a lot to learn about the pack.

But there was another wolf who was especially interested in the pups—one we never expected. Amani, the wolf who had bullied Lakota, adored the pups!

Amani romped gently around the little black balls of fur. He lay down and let them climb on him and nip his ears. He even let them play tug with his tail! He never got tired of them. Amani was a different wolf with the pups—a gentle uncle.

We knew that the end of summer would come quickly. And so would our permission to stay on the land. Because these wolves had been raised with people, they weren't afraid of humans. They didn't know that they needed to avoid the danger of hunters. We had to find the right place for the wolves. We spoke to a Native American tribe, the Nez Perce, in northern Idaho. They agreed the pack could live on their land.

We gave the Sawtooth pups names in the tribe's language. We called the male Piyip (sounds like pie-YIP), which means "boy." The females we named Ayet (sounds like eye-YET), which means "girl" and Motaki, after the wolf that had been killed by the cougar. We knew the pack would be safe, but it was still hard to say goodbye!

Wolves in the Sawtooth Today

Years after we left the territory, Jim and I decided to return. It was late fall, and the ground was muddy. There was a sprinkling of snow, too. Nothing was left of wolf camp. As we walked along, we noticed paw prints but didn't think anything of it. After all, we'd seen wolf tracks here for years. Then we stopped. These tracks meant that a wolf had walked through recently. We were overjoyed. Wild wolves were in the Sawtooth mountains again!

THE END

DON'T MISS!

NATIONAL GEOGRAPHIC KiDS **CHAPTERS**

RHINO RESCUE!

And More True Stories of Saving Animals

Clare Hodgson Meeker

**Turn the page
for a sneak preview . . .**

KASS AND DRAEGON: RHINO RESCUE!

A helicopter flies low over several rhinoceroses to see if they might be good candidates for the airlift.

A mother rhinoceros and her calf walk along the grassland in search of a watering hole.

Chapter 1

Thinking BIG

February 2015
South Africa

The day was hot and muggy on the African savanna. A female white rhinoceros nibbled hungrily on some tufts of grass. Beside her, her young calf shook off a pesky fly. The fly was circling above the two small horns on the calf's nose. Mother and son rhino ambled along in the tall grass.

They had wallowed in mud earlier at the watering hole to cool their skin. Now mud-caked, they paused for a moment in the baking sun. All was quiet.

Suddenly, the sound of a helicopter cut through the hazy sky. The mother rhino lifted her head. A rhino has poor vision, but can hear sounds that are very far away. She could not tell where this noise was coming from, though.

The calf stood still and watched as his mother looked anxiously around. The sound grew closer and louder. Was this sound a threat? A rhino's natural instinct is to avoid danger.

Did You Know?

Rhinoceroses have thick but sensitive skin. That's why they like to wallow in mud. When the mud dries, it protects their skin from insects.

But there was nowhere to hide. The rhinos began to run.

There was no way for the rhinos to know that they were not in danger. There was no way for them to know that they were actually being rescued. A veterinarian (sounds like vet-er-ih-NAIR-ee-en) and a pilot were aboard the helicopter. They're part of a group called Rhinos Without Borders.

This group has a bold plan to protect rhinos from poachers and help prevent rhino extinction (sounds like ek-STINK-shun). Rhinos are in serious trouble. There are fewer than 22,000 of them in the world. More than 1,000 African rhinos are shot and killed by poachers each year.

Rhinos

There are five rhino species on Earth. Two of the species that live in Africa are the black rhino and the white rhino. Both of these rhinoceros species are actually gray. They are different not in color, but in the shape of their lips. The black rhino has a pointed upper lip. The white rhino has a squared lip. This difference is related to what the animals eat. Black rhinos are

white rhino

browsers. They get most of their food from trees and bushes. They use their upper lips to grab leaves, twigs, and fruit. White rhinos graze on grasses. They walk with their enormous heads and squared lips lowered to the ground. The white rhino's name came from mispronouncing the Dutch word *wyd* (sounds like WIDE) to describe its upper lip.

Poachers cut off rhino horns and sell them for thousands of dollars. The people who buy the horns grind them up for "medicine" or make them into dagger handles. At the rate rhinos are being killed, there will be no free-roaming rhinos in Africa within five years.

That's where National Geographic Explorers Dereck and Beverly Joubert (sounds like jhoo-BEAR) come in.

The Jouberts are award-winning filmmakers who have been filming, researching, and exploring in Africa for more than 30 years. Their mission is to save the wild places of Africa and to protect the creatures that depend on them.

Over time, the Jouberts have learned how important all animals are to the land. In 2009, the Jouberts founded the "Big Cats Initiative" with National Geographic.

This program aims to stop the rapid decline of wild cats—like lions, leopards, tigers, jaguars, and cheetahs—around the world. The program has seen a lot of success. Now the Jouberts wanted to use what they learned with Big Cats to help save the African rhino.

South Africa has more rhinos than any other country in Africa. South Africa also has more poachers. The Jouberts came up with a daring plan . . .

Want to know what happens next? Be sure to check out *Rhino Rescue!*

INDEX

Boldface indicates illustrations.

Alpha wolf, role of 21–23, 31, 41, 78–79, 82

Beta wolf, role of 62, 66, 75–76

Conservationists 74
Cougars 10, 12, 44–46

Deer 42, 45, 94
Dogs 10, 64

Ecosystems 77
Elk 42, 45–46, 77, **77**
Ethiopian wolves 64

Fairy tales 12

Geladas 64
Gray wolves
    fur colors 40
    undercoat 61
    weight 11
Greek alphabet 50
Grizzly bears 93

Hunters 16, 64, 74, 84, 85, 97

Leptocyon 66
Living With Wolves (organization) 85

Monkeys 64
Moose 23, 45, 73

Nez Perce 97

Omega wolf, role of 41, 49, 51, 52, 67, 78

Predators 43, 93

Ranchers 16, 84
Regurgitated food 88
Roman myth 63

Sawtooth Pack: family history 4–5
Sawtooth Range, Idaho 14, 15, **28,** 60, 84, 98
Social animals 11

Wolverines 16
Wolves
    bite force 73
    body language 39, 50–51
    dens 82–83, 88, 91–95
    hearing 23, 87
    how to help 85
    howling **6–7,** 24, **24,** 26, 33, 35
    layers of fur 60–61
    paws 55, **55**
    personalities 49, 50, 61
    prey 13, 20, 42, 64
    sense of smell 44
    teeth 20, 88

Yellowstone National Park, U.S. 74, 93
Yurts 14–15, **28**

MORE INFORMATION

livingwithwolves.org

The website for Jim and Jamie's nonprofit organization, Living With Wolves, is dedicated to educational outreach. Learn more about how dogs evolved from wolves, how wolves help ecosystems, their family bonds, and threats to their survival. Plus find other stories about the Sawtooth Pack.

Additional educator resources and lesson plans:

education.nationalgeographic.org/media/jim-jamie-dutcher-hidden-life-wolves/

A collection of science and social studies resources for grades 6–12 about Jim and Jamie's work with wolves

education.nationalgeographic.org/media/wolf-language

Information about wolf communication

education.nationalgeographic.org/media/gray-wolf-educator-guide/

Exploring a keystone species with students in grades K–12

education.nationalgeographic.org/media/gray-wolf-family-activity-guide/

Exploring curiosity about the natural world with children ages 4–10

Other National Geographic books by Jim and Jamie:
The Hidden Life of Wolves, 2013
A Friend for Lakota, 2015

CREDITS

For our grandchildren—Arianna, Sofia, Natalie, Sebastian, and Emiko—and children all around the world. Together we can make a difference for wolves and the natural world. The future is in your hands. —J & J

ACKNOWLEDGMENTS

Jim and Jamie wish to offer their appreciation to the following people: We would like to thank Moira Donohue, who believed in our story and added so much. To Garrick Dutcher, Kris Stoffer, Sheryl Schowengerdt, Patricia Kilmartin, and Laverne Berry for their dedication to Living With Wolves. Shelby Alinsky, Brenna Maloney, and Jeff Heimsath for their vision, hard work, and skill in producing this book. And a special thank-you to our five grandchildren for their input and whom we love more than words can express.

AUTHOR'S NOTE

Jim and Jamie Dutcher and their team are professional wildlife experts. They've spent many years learning about wolves, and that means they know how to keep safe around them. For most people, though, approaching a wild animal can be dangerous. So, remember: If you see a wolf in the wild, count yourself very lucky, but keep your distance!